W9-AYN-639

JAMES
BEARD'S
SOUPS

JAMES BEARD'S SOUPS

EDITED BY JOHN FERRONE

THAMES AND HUDSON
New York, New York

First published in the United States of America in paperback in 1997 by Thames and Hudson Inc., 500 Fifth Avenue, New York, New York, 10110

Library of Congress Catalog Card Number 97–60239
ISBN 0–500–27968–3

Designed, typeset and produced by Liz Trovato Book Design
Cover illustration by Patricia Pardini

Printed and bound in Mexico

EDITOR'S NOTE

All of the recipes and much of the text in this cookbook series are James Beard's and are gathered from many sources—magazine articles, syndicated columns, cookbooks, cooking lessons--covering thirty years of culinary exploration. The choice of recipes gives a fair sampling of his thinking on a variety of foods and cuisines. Although he is associated primarily with American cookery, Beard was always on the lookout for gastronomic inspiration in other parts of the world. These cookbooks offer dishes from Portland to Paris, from Maryland to Mexico. Many of them are Beard favorites that turned up in his cooking classes and cookbooks through the years, but also included are less familiar dishes that deserve to be better known. Recipes and text have been edited for these special editions.

BEARD ON SOUPS

Time was when every dinner had to include a soup, and in some great households there was always a choice of thick or clear. Consommé was a menu standard, and clarified chicken and veal stocks were always kept on hand in vast quantities. Soup, moreover, was never served at lunch, only at dinner, a rule certainly no longer observed.

Nowadays if soup is served it is likely to be something inventive and unusual. Many cooks of my acquaintance like to take an idea, adapt it, and give it their signature. The smallest variation on a familiar recipe can turn it into a specialty.

Although a good strong stock is the base for most successful soups, from consommé onward, few home kitchens can accommodate great simmering cauldrons of bones and meat, or store two or three gallons of stock, to be drawn as needed. We have learned to depend on other, speedier sources for our stocks. The ready availability of chicken parts enables us to prepare a chicken stock in a relatively short time, using the less desirable parts of the bird and discarding them after all the goodness has been extracted.

For Chicken Stock: In a large kettle combine 4 pounds of chicken backs and necks, 2 pounds of chicken gizzards, 4 quarts of water, 1 onion stuck with 2 cloves, 1 rib of celery, a few peppercorns, 1 teaspoon of thyme, 2 or 3 sprigs of parsley, and salt to taste. Bring the liquid to a boil and boil for 5 minutes, skimming the froth from the surface as it rises. Reduce the heat and simmer, covered, for 3 to 4 hours. Strain it, taste for seasoning, and let it cool.

A stock made with oxtails is a delightful change from the more usual beef stock. The texture is richer and the flavor more distinguished. For Oxtail Consommé: Arrange 3 oxtails, cut in sections, on the rack of a broiling pan about 4 inches from the broiling unit. Broil the pieces, turning them once or twice, until they are well browned on all sides and crisp at the edges. Transfer them to an 8-quart kettle and add 1 veal knuckle, 3 carrots, cut into strips, 3 leeks, well cleaned, 1 onion stuck with 2 cloves, 1 bay leaf, 1 tablespoon of salt, 1 teaspoon of rosemary, 8 to 10 peppercorns, and 4 quarts of water. Bring to a boil and boil rapidly for 5 minutes, skimming the froth from the surface. Reduce the heat, cover the pan, and simmer the soup for 2 to 3 hours. Strain. Taste for seasoning. Let cool overnight and remove the fat.

Occasionally, at a great dinner where the chef revels in doing a superb job, one encounters a clear soup that is truly remarkable. I recall such a one at a fabled dinner given many years ago in New York. The consommé was made of turkey, or rather a succession of turkeys, with one bird replacing another in the stock until the essence of six turkeys had been concentrated into one soup. What made it all the more remarkable was the fact that it was not seasoned at all. The flavor came from the natural salt and seasoning in the birds themselves. Slow, careful cooking, accurate timing, and painstaking clarification made this one of the best clear soups I had ever tasted.

—JAMES BEARD

CONTENTS

Hearty Soups

Vegetable Soups

Seafood Soups

Cold Soups

HEARTY
SOUPS

BEEF BORSCHT

There are even more ways to prepare this Russian dish than there are spellings of its name (also Borsht and Borsch). This meaty version is hardy enough to serve as a one-dish meal.

3 quarts beef broth
2 cups diced cooked beef
4 small raw beets, shredded
4 potatoes, peeled and thinly sliced
2 medium onions, coarsely chopped
2 cups finely shredded raw cabbage
¼ to ½ cup lemon juice
2 or 3 tablespoons sugar

Bring the broth to a boil in a large pot. Add the shredded beets, cover, and simmer for 15 minutes. Add the rest of the veg-etables and cook until they are quite soft. Add the lemon juice, starting with ¼ cup, then add 2 tablespoons of sugar. Add more lemon juice or sugar until there is a nice sweet-sour balance. Finally add the diced beef and heat through. Serve in large bowls or soup plates along with black bread and sweet butter.

VARIATION:

For cold Borscht, omit the diced beef. When the vegetables are done, drain off the broth into a bowl. Puree the vegetables and combine again with the broth. Allow to cool, then refrigerate until thoroughly chilled. Serve in bowls with a spoonful of sour cream.

GARBURE BASQUAISE

Serves 6 to 8

This hearty and delicious Basque soup is almost a stew, combining dried legumes, vegetables, and sausages. It is just the thing for a cold-weather supper, and it is also a good way to use up the end of a ham.

1 pound white pea beans
½ pound dried peas
1 meaty ham knuckle
3 bay leaves
1 onion, stuck with 2 cloves
3 quarts water
6 potatoes, cut into small pieces
4 to 5 carrots, sliced
4 turnips, cut into small pieces
4 to 5 leeks, cut up
6 cloves garlic, chopped
1 teaspoon dried thyme
1 small head of cabbage, shredded
12 to 16 small sausages
Grated Swiss cheese

Naturally you will use quick-cooking beans and peas for this dish. Put them in a deep pot with water to cover, bring to a boil, then turn off the heat and let stand for 1 hour. Drain, and return to the pot with the ham knuckle, 2 of the bay leaves, the onion and the 3 quarts of water. Bring to a boil, reduce the heat, and simmer for about 1 hour or until the legumes are tender but not mushy. Taste for salt; you may not need to add any if the ham is salty. Drain the beans and ham and keep them warm. Pour the liquid back into the pot.

Add the potatoes, carrots, turnips, leeks, garlic, thyme, and remaining bay leaf, and cook until the vegetables are tender. Meanwhile prick the sausages to release the fat, pre-cook them in water for 10 minutes, and drain. Finally add the cabbage to the pot, along with the beans, the meat from the ham bone, and the sausages. Cook until the cabbage is just done. The soup should be very thick.

Dish it into ovenproof bowls, top with toast and grated Swiss cheese, and put under the broiler for a minute to glaze the cheese. Or simply sprinkle with cheese and eat with plenty of French bread.

To make the garbure even more flavorful add leftover cooked chicken, duck, or goose. Grill the sausages and serve separately. Make the garbure with pigs' knuckles instead of ham bone.

CHICKEN-NOODLE SOUP

Makes about 2½ quarts

This simple, comforting soup has been a kitchen staple for generations. It is best made with a stewing fowl, which is worth the long cooking time it requires but is hard to find these days. A roasting chicken makes an acceptable substitute.

One 4- to 5-pound stewing fowl or
   roasting chicken
3 quarts water
1 medium onion, peeled
1 stalk celery
1 sprig parsley
1 tablespoon salt
6 peppercorns
4 ounces egg noodles

Put the chicken into a deep pot with the water, vegetables, parsley, and seasonings. Bring to a boil and skim off any scum that forms. Reduce the heat, cover, and simmer gently until the chicken is tender—2 to 2½ hours for a fowl, about 1 hour for a young roaster. Remove the chicken from the broth. As soon as it has cooled, strip off the skin and cut the meat into dice or small pieces. Return the carcass to the broth and cook another 45 minutes, then strain the broth through cheesecloth or a linen napkin. Allow to cool until the fat rises to the top. Skim off the excess fat. (This is more easily done if the soup is made a day ahead and the broth can be completely chilled.)

Cook the noodles in boiling salted water until just tender. Drain. Reheat the broth, taste for seasoning, and add the chicken pieces and noodles. Serve steaming hot in large bowls.

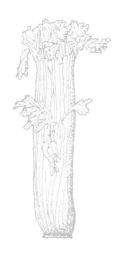

PEPPER POT

A soup that originated in Philadelphia and is supposed to have Dutch roots, but it could easily have come from the tripe-loving English or French.

1 veal knuckle
1 leek, cleaned and sliced
Sprig of parsley
Sprig of thyme or 1/2 teaspoon dried
1 bay leaf
3 quarts water
4 pounds cooked tripe, cut into
*   small cubes*
2 onions, chopped
1 tablespoon salt
1 1/2 teaspoons freshly ground black
*   pepper*
1 or 2 hot red peppers or 1 teaspoon
*   Tabasco*
1/2 pound beef suet, finely chopped
2 cups flour
4 or 5 potatoes, peeled and diced
2 tablespoons chopped parsley

Place the veal knuckle, leek, and herbs in a deep pot with the water. Bring to a boil, skim off any scum that forms, then cover and simmer for 2 1/2 hours. Remove the veal knuckle, take the meat from the bone, and cut it into small pieces. Strain the broth. Return to the pot, and add the veal, tripe, chopped onions, seasoning, and red peppers or Tabasco. Cover and simmer for 1 1/2 hours. Meanwhile blend the suet and flour together with a little water to make a doughy paste. Form into tiny balls and drop into the simmering soup to thicken it. Add the potatoes and chopped parsley, and cook for another hour. Taste for seasoning. Serve with toast.

SCOTCH BROTH

The ingredients of this long-time favorite can vary a good deal, and it is often made with lamb or mutton instead of beef.

2 pounds shin of beef
1/4 pound pearl barley
1 large bunch parsley, tied
4 quarts water
1 tablespoon salt or to taste
1/2 teaspoon pepper
4 onions, sliced
6 medium potatoes, cubed
Chopped parsley

Combine the beef, barley, parsley, and water in a large pot. Bring to a boil, cover, and simmer 1 hour. Add salt and pepper, and continue cooking for another hour. Add the onions and potatoes and simmer for a final hour. Taste for seasoning.

Remove the meat and parsley. Slice the meat and distribute among individual bowls. Add the soup and sprinkle with chopped parsley.

LENTIL SOUP

Lentils might have been designed for winter meals. They are marvelously satisfying and nutritious, and their flavor is more distinctive than that of any other bean, except perhaps the fava. Thanks to processed packaged lentils, long soaking and cooking is no longer required, and lentils can be prepared in very little time. They are seldom better than in a hearty soup.

1 pound lentils
2 to 3 quarts water or broth
Ham bone
Salt and freshly ground black
*   pepper*
1 cup finely chopped onions
2 finely chopped garlic cloves
1 teaspoon dried thyme
¼ teaspoon nutmeg
Chopped parsley
Crisp croutons

Put the lentils in a deep pot with the water and ham bone. Bring to a boil, cover, and cook until the lentils are very soft, about 1 hour. Put the lentils through a food mill or puree in a food processor. Taste for salt and add freshly ground black pepper. Add the onions, garlic, thyme, nutmeg, and enough water or broth to make a good thick soup. Simmer for another 30 minutes. Taste again for seasoning, and serve, garnishing each portion with chopped parsley and croutons.

VARIATION:

Add thinly sliced frankfurters or knackwurst for the last 5 to 10 minutes of cooking. Stir in ½ cup heavy cream for the last 5 minutes.

LENTIL, CHARD, AND LEMON SOUP
(ADAS BI HAAMUD)

Serves 6

This is a tart, Syrian version of lentil soup. It can also be served cold.

1 1/2 cups lentils

2 1/2 pounds fresh Swiss chard

1/2 cup olive oil

3/4 cup chopped onion

3 to 4 cloves garlic, crushed
    in 1/2 teaspoon salt

Salt and freshly ground black
    pepper

1 stalk celery, chopped

1/2 cup lemon juice, mixed with
    1 teaspoon flour

Put the lentils in a pot with enough cold water to more than cover. Bring to a boil, cover, and simmer until tender, about 30 to 45 minutes. Wash the chard, and coarsely chop. Add to the lentils with another cup of water. Simmer until the chard is wilted.

Heat the oil in a skillet, and add the onions, garlic, and celery. Sauté until tender and blended, then add to the lentils. Stir in the lemon juice. Continue cooking until the soup has thickened. Taste for seasoning. Serve with crusty bread.

SPINACH AND CHICK PEA SOUP

Serves 8

Chick peas, also known as garbanzos, need long cooking to tenderize them, so in this case it is best to use canned ones, which have been processed and are ready to eat.

8 cups beef broth
2 cups canned chick peas, drained
1 cup chopped carrots
1 cup chopped onions
1 cup chopped celery
1 cup chopped turnips
1 cup coarsely chopped spinach
2 cups canned or stewed tomatoes
Grated Parmesan

Pour the broth into a deep pot, and add the chick peas, carrots, onions, celery, and turnips. Simmer for 20 to 30 minutes. Add the spinach and tomatoes and simmer a few minutes longer. Taste for seasoning. Serve sprinkled with grated Parmesan.

BLACK BEAN SOUP

Serves 12

A plebeian soup that achieved great distinction in this version, served at the former Coach House restaurant in New York.

2 cups black beans

4 tablespoons butter

2 large onions, coarsely chopped

2 garlic cloves, crushed

3 leeks, well cleaned and cut into
    1/2-inch pieces

1 celery stalk, coarsely chopped

2 bay leaves

2 cloves

1 ham shank, split

3 pounds beef or veal bones

2 tablespoons flour

4 to 5 quarts water

Salt to taste

8 peppercorns

1/2 cup Madeira

GARNISH:

Chopped parsley, 2 finely chopped
    hard-boiled eggs, thin lemon slices

Either soak the beans overnight or put in a pot with water to more than cover, bring to a boil, and let stand for 1 hour. Drain.

Melt the butter in a deep pot, and sauté the vegetables for about 3 minutes. Add the bay leaves, cloves, ham shank, and bones, and cook another 3 or 4 minutes. Blend in the flour. Cook 2 or 3 minutes. Stir in the water, salt, and peppercorns and bring to a boil. Skim off any scum that forms, then reduce the heat, cover loosely, and simmer about 8 hours. Add the beans, and simmer 2½ hours more, stirring from time to time and adding more water if needed.

Remove from the heat, extract the ham shank, and discard the bones. Puree the beans and vegetables in a food mill or food processor. Return to the pot and taste for seasoning. Stir in the Madeira, and bring to boil. Serve garnished with parsley, chopped hard-boiled eggs, and lemon slices.

VEGETABLE
SOUPS

OLD-TIME
VEGETABLE SOUP

Serves 6 to 8

There is no fixed recipe for vegetable soup, and the contents can be varied infinitely according to taste and the ingredients at hand. Followed by a substantial salad and a good dessert, this recipe makes a satisfying vegetarian meal.

2 quarts beef broth
2 carrots, finely diced
2 turnips, finely diced
3 large onions, finely chopped
2 cloves garlic, finely chopped
1 cup fresh or frozen peas
1 cup fresh or frozen lima beans
One 29-ounce can tomatoes
¼ cup finely chopped parsley
1½ cups small pasta or
    pasta broken into small piece
Grated Parmesan cheese

Put the broth, carrots, turnips, onions, and garlic into a pot and simmer for 25 minutes. Add the peas, beans, tomatoes, parsley, and pasta, and cook for another 15 minutes. (Or cook the pasta separately in boiling salted water and add last.) Taste for seasoning. Serve in large bowls, and pass the Parmesan cheese.

CREAM OF
ASPARAGUS SOUP

Serves 4

This recipe can be adapted to make almost any cream vegetable soup, replacing the asparagus with 1 cup of finely chopped vegetable, such as cauliflower, celery, or broccoli.

2 cups chicken broth
1 cup chopped asparagus
1 small onion, finely chopped
1 tablespoon butter
¼ cup chopped parsley
1 cup heavy cream or half-and-half
1 or 2 teaspoons arrowroot
Salt and freshly ground black pepper
Chopped chives or chopped parsley

Pour the broth in a pot and add the asparagus. Lightly sauté the onion in the butter, and also add to the broth along with the parsley. Bring to a boil, cover, and simmer until the asparagus is tender. Drain the broth into a bowl. Put the vegetables through a food mill or puree in a food processor. Combine with the broth, and return to the pot. Stir in the cream or half-and-half over low heat. Mix the arrowroot with a little milk, and stir into the broth. Continue stirring until the soup thickens and comes to a boil. Taste for seasoning. Serve with chopped chives or chopped parsley.

CREAM OF ARTICHOKE SOUP

Serves 4

One of the rarer cream of vegetable soups, which takes a bit more work but is well worth the time spent scraping artichoke leaves.

2 cups chicken broth
2 good-sized artichokes
(approximately)
1 small onion peeled and chopped
2 tablespoons chopped parsley
Salt and freshly ground black pepper
1 cup heavy cream or half-and-half

Boil the artichokes in salted water until the tips of the leaves are soft to the bite when tested, about 40 minutes. Take apart the artichokes and discard the chokes. Scrape the flesh from the leaves with a spoon, trim the bottoms, and cut off the top of the tender inner section or "heart." Puree in a blender or food processor. You will need 1 cup.

Put the broth, artichoke puree, chopped onion and chopped parsley in a sauce-pan and bring to a boil. Stir in the cream or half-and-half, and gradually reheat. If you are using the latter, you may need to thicken the soup. A touch of instant mashed potato will do the trick. Taste for seasoning. Serve sprinkled with chopped chives or parsley.

CREAM OF TOMATO SOUP

Serves 4 to 6

An easy soup that is distinctive enough to serve to company. This was the recipe used in the Beard household for many years.

3 cups canned tomatoes

1 cup beef broth

1 small onion, stuck with 2 cloves

1 teaspoon salt

1/2 teaspoon freshly ground black pepper

1 teaspoon dried basil

1 1/2 teaspoons sugar

1/4 teaspoon bicarbonate of soda

1 1/2 tablespoons flour

1 1/2 tablespoons butter

2 cups heavy cream

Chopped parsley or chopped fresh basil

Put the tomatoes, broth, onion, seasoning, and basil in a saucepan. Cover and simmer over low heat for 30 minutes. Add the sugar, and cook for another 10 minutes. Remove the cloves from the onion, and put the vegetables through a food mill or puree in a food processor. Add the baking soda. Taste for seasoning. Blend the butter and flour together into a smooth paste, and stir it into the tomato mixture over medium heat. Cook until slightly thickened. Remove from the heat. In a separate saucepan bring the heavy cream almost to a boil. Gradually stir into the tomato puree. Bring nearly to a boil over low heat. Serve with a sprinkling of parsley or basil.

CREAM OF MUSHROOM SOUP

Serves 6 to 8

Canned cream of mushroom soup has acquired a bad name in American cooking through misuse as a sauce. Freshly made mushroom soup is quite another matter.

1 pound fresh mushrooms

1 quart chicken broth

2 tablespoons butter

3 tablespoons flour

2 tablespoons medium sherry
   or cognac

2 cups heavy cream

Salt

1/4 teaspoon Tabasco

Clean the mushrooms well. Remove the stems and slice the caps. Put the stems in a saucepan with the broth, and simmer for 35 to 40 minutes. Strain the broth into a bowl. Discard the stems. Melt the butter in the saucepan, stir in the flour for a minute or so, and then gradually stir in the broth. Cook over medium heat until slightly thickened. Add the sliced mushrooms, and simmer another 8 to 10 minutes. Stir in the sherry or cognac, the cream, and the Tabasco, and heat through. Taste for salt.

CURRIED PEA SOUP

Serves 4

The spiciness of the curry gives an otherwise ordinary pea soup a wonderful lift. Frozen peas are called for here, but an equivalent amount of fresh peas would be even better.

1 package frozen peas
1 medium onion, peeled and sliced
1 small carrot, peeled and sliced
1 garlic clove, peeled
1 stalk celery, with a bit of
    the leaves, chopped
1 medium potato, peeled and cubed
1 teaspoon curry
2 cups chicken broth
Salt
1 cup heavy cream

Put the vegetables, curry and 1 cup of the broth in a saucepan. Bring to a boil, cover, and reduce the heat. Simmer for 15 minutes. Put through a food mill or puree in a blender or food processor. Stir in the remaining broth and the cream. Gently reheat. Taste for salt. Serve hot or chill and serve cold.

POTATO AND LEEK SOUP

Serves 6 to 8

One of the simplest and most enduring of soup recipes. It is perhaps best known in its cold version, as Vichyssoise.

5 or 6 leeks
5 tablespoons butter
3 cups diced potatoes
1 quart chicken broth
Salt to taste
Pinch cayenne
Pinch nutmeg
2 tablespoons flour

Split the leeks lengthwise, and wash well to remove all grit. Cut crosswise into slices. Sauté gently in the butter for 3 or 4 minutes, but do not allow to brown. Transfer to a pot, and add the potatoes and broth. Bring to a boil, cover, and simmer until the potatoes are tender, about 20 minutes. Drain the vegetables and reserve the broth. Put the vegetables through a food mill or puree in a food processor. Return to the soup pot, and stir in the broth. Add salt, if needed—the chicken broth may be salty enough—and cayenne and nutmeg to taste. In a separate saucepan melt the remaining butter over low heat, and stir in the flour. Blend in 1½ cups of the soup and heat till thickened. Stir back into the soup pot. Bring to a boil and serve.

VARIATION:

For Vichyssoise, allow the soup to cool, then blend in 1½ cups heavy cream. Chill thoroughly and serve with a sprinkling of chopped chives.

ONION SOUP

A soup that traveled from France to America more than a century and a half ago and has been popular ever since.

6 medium onions, peeled and sliced
Beef or bacon fat
6 cups beef broth
3 ounces dry sherry
6 slices toasted French bread
Grated Swiss cheese
Grated Parmesan cheese

Sauté the onions in the fat until lightly browned and tender. Add the broth and sherry, and simmer for 15 minutes. Ladle into oven-proof bowls, top with a slice of toast, and sprinkle with the grated cheeses. Put into a 350° oven for 10 minutes or until the cheese melts and forms a light crust.

VARIATIONS:

• Sauté the onions in butter and oil instead of fat.
• Use 1 cup red wine or port instead of sherry.
• Omit the Swiss cheese, and simply serve with grated Parmesan and toast.

GARLIC SOUP

Serves 6 to 8

Don't be alarmed by the quantity of garlic called for here. After garlic has been cooked slowly for a certain length of time it loses its harshness and becomes quite delicate. The beautiful flavor of this soup is something that could never be achieved with garlic powder. So don't even think about it.

3 tablespoons fat—preferably chicken, goose, or pork
30 peeled garlic cloves, more or less, to taste
6 to 8 cups chicken broth
Salt and freshly ground black pepper
Pinch freshly grated nutmeg
4 or 5 egg yolks
3 to 4 tablespoons olive oil
Crisp toast

Melt the fat in a heavy saucepan over low heat. Add the garlic and cook gently, shaking the pan often, so that it softens in the fat without browning. (Browning will make the flavor bitter.) Add the chicken broth and season to taste with salt, pepper, and nutmeg. Simmer for 15 to 20 minutes, then drain the garlic—reserving the broth—and put through a food mill or puree in a food processor. Return the garlic and broth to the saucepan and reheat. Beat the egg yolks and stir the olive oil into them. Blend a little of the soup into the mixture to temper the eggs, then stir all very gently back into the soup. Heat thoroughly, but do not allow to boil or the yolks will curdle. Place a piece of toast in each soup plate and ladle the soup over it.

PUMPKIN
AND GINGER SOUP

Serves 6

A new role for pumpkin on the holiday dinner menu. The soup can be made more substantial with a garnish of finely diced or slivered baked country ham.

2 pounds pumpkin or other
  winter squash
1 onion, stuck with 2 cloves
3 cups chicken broth
1/4 teaspoon cinnamon
1/4 teaspoon freshly ground black
  pepper
2 tablespoons chopped fresh ginger
Salt
1 cup heavy cream or yogurt

Peel and trim the pumpkin or squash and cut it into cubes. Place in a saucepan with the onion, broth, spices, and ginger. Bring to a boil, cover, and simmer over low heat until the pumpkin is very tender. Discard the onion. Drain off the broth and reserve. Put the pumpkin and ginger through a food mill or puree in a food processor. Return to the saucepan and stir in the broth. Taste for salt. Add the heavy cream or yogurt, and stir at a simmer until heated through. Stop well short of a boil if using yogurt.

AVGOLEMONO
(EGG-LEMON SOUP)

One of the best-known and most delicious of Greek dishes. It requires few ingredients but depends on egg yolks for thickening and must be made with great care.

8 cups rich chicken broth
½ cup uncooked rice
Salt
2 whole eggs
2 egg yolks
Juice of 2 lemons, about ½ cup

Bring the broth to a boil in a saucepan, add the rice, and cook until tender, about 20 minutes. Taste for salt, and add if necessary. Beat the whole eggs and yolks together until light and frothy, and slowly beat in the lemon juice. Blend a cup of the hot broth, a little at a time, into the egg-lemon mixture to temper the eggs and prevent them from curdling. Then very slowly add this to the rest of the broth over low heat, stirring constantly, until slightly thickened. Do not allow to come to a boil.

SEAFOOD
SOUPS

SPINACH AND SEAFOOD SOUP

Serves 8

An unusual cold soup in which the ingredients are cooked separately, then assembled and thickened with mashed potatoes.

3 pounds fresh spinach

2 quarts well-flavored fat-free
    chicken broth

Juice of 1 lemon

1 tablespoon chopped fresh tarragon
    or 1 teaspoon dried

1 clove of garlic, finely chopped

Salt to taste

1 teaspoon freshly ground black
    pepper

¾ cup cold mashed potatoes

1 cup finely chopped cooked shrimp,
    crabmeat or lobster

½ cup sour cream

2 tablespoons chopped parsley

Wash the spinach well and put it in a pot with just the water clinging to its leaves. Cover and cook over medium heat until just wilted. Drain and squeeze to remove excess moisture. Chop as finely as possible. Put it in a large bowl with the broth, lemon juice, tarragon, garlic, salt (depending on the salt content of the broth) and pepper. Mix well, then beat in just enough of the mashed potato to give the soup a smooth, slightly thickened consistency. Chill well. Pour the soup into chilled bowls, and add 2 tablespoons of chopped seafood to each portion. Top with sour cream and a sprinkling of parsley.

NEW ENGLAND FISH CHOWDER

Serves 4

Every country has its fish soups and stews. Chowders are America's contribution, and the most popular of all is Clam Chowder. Fish Chowder is made exactly the same way, substituting flaked fish for clams. As any New Englander will tell you, genuine old-fashioned chowder is never made with tomatoes.

¼ cup diced salt pork
¼ cup sliced onions
2 cups diced potatoes
2 cups hot water
1½ pounds haddock or cod fillets
Salt and freshly ground black pepper
2 cups light cream
Butter

Sauté the salt pork in a large skillet until it has rendered most of its fat and is browned and crisp. Add the onions and cook gently until tender. Then add the potatoes and hot water. Cook until the potatoes are nearly done. Add the fish fillets and cook until just done. Break into flakes with two forks.

Season with salt and pepper to taste. Stir in the cream. Heat through. Serve in bowls with a dab of butter in each.

QUICK CLAM CHOWDER

Serves 4

A recipe that can be put together on the spur of the moment if you happen to have canned clams and evaporated milk on the shelf and a few slices of bacon in the larder.

Two 7-ounce cans minced clams
2 medium potatoes, peeled and diced
3 or 4 slices salt pork or bacon, diced
1 medium onion, peeled and chopped
Salt and freshly ground black pepper
2 cups light cream or evaporated
  milk
Pinch of thyme
Paprika

Drain the liquid from the clams, and reserve. Boil the potatoes in lightly salted water until nearly done. Lift out the potatoes and set aside. Cook down the potato water for a few minutes. Fry the salt pork or bacon in a skillet until crisp.

Transfer to paper towels while you gently sauté the onion in the pork or bacon fat until limp. Do not brown. Add the salt pork or bacon, onion, potatoes, and reserved clam liquor to the potato water. Bring to a boil, reduce the heat, and simmer for 5 to 10 minutes. Season with salt and pepper, and gradually stir in the cream or evaporated milk and the minced clams. Slowly heat just to the boiling point. Stir in the thyme. Serve with a sprinkling of paprika.

CULLEN SKINK

A great Scottish soup that is a subtle mixture of potatoes, leeks, and smoked haddock or finnan haddie. Its cold version becomes a Scottish Vichyssoise.

3 medium to large potatoes
1½ quarts water
2 or 3 leeks
½ to ¾ pound finnan haddie
Salt and freshly ground black pepper
Pinch freshly grated nutmeg
4 to 5 tablespoons butter
Chopped parsley

Peel the potatoes. Trim the leeks, cut in half lengthwise, and rinse well to remove the sand. Then cut into small pieces. Put the potatoes and leeks in a saucepan with the water and just a touch of salt (the finnan haddie will be salty). Boil until the potatoes are tender. Remove them and put through a food mill or potato ricer. Add the finnan haddie to the pot, and poach gently until it flakes easily, about 10 to 15 minutes. Remove the fish and puree two-thirds of it in a food mill or food processor, setting aside the rest. Combine the pureed fish with the potatoes, and return to the saucepan. Bring slowly to a boil while stirring until the potatoes have thickened the broth. Taste for seasoning and add the nutmeg. Stir in the butter. Crumble the remaining finnan haddie, and add just before serving. Ladle into soup bowls and sprinkle with chopped parsley.

VARIATIONS:

For a richer, creamier soup, stir in ½ to 1 cup heavy cream after thickening with the potatoes, and let it come to a boil.

To serve cold: Puree all of the finnan haddie and leeks instead of reserving some, and proceed with the recipe. When the soup is done, allow it to cool, then refrigerate overnight. Just before serving, stir in ½ to 1 cup heavy cream. Sprinkle with chopped chives or chopped parsley.

CIOPPINO

A hearty fish soup that also qualifies as a stew. It was invented by California fishermen—so the story goes— who used whatever seafood was at hand. There is no fixed recipe and this is one of many.

1 quart of clams or mussels

3 cups red wine, such as Pinot Noir

1/2 cup olive oil

1 large onion, chopped

2 cloves garlic, chopped

1 green pepper, chopped

1/4 pound dried mushrooms, rehydrated in warm water, drained and chopped

4 ripe tomatoes, peeled, seeded, and chopped

4 tablespoons Italian tomato paste

2 teaspoons salt

1 teaspoon freshly ground black pepper

2 tablespoons finely chopped fresh basil or 1 teaspoon dried

3 pounds thick fish fillets, cut into serving pieces

1 pound cooked crabmeat

1 pound raw shrimp, shelled

3 tablespoons chopped parsley

Put the clams or mussels in a pan with 1 cup of the wine, cover, and steam until they open. Discard any that do not. Strain off the broth through cheesecloth into a bowl and set aside. Heat the oil in an 8-quart pot, add the onion, garlic, pepper, and rehydrated mushrooms, and sauté gently for 3 minutes.

Add the tomatoes, cook another 4 minutes, then add the reserved broth, tomato paste, remaining wine, and salt and pepper. Simmer over low heat for 20 minutes. Taste for salt. Add the fresh or dried basil and the pieces of fish. Simmer for 3 to 5 minutes or until the fish is just cooked through. Add the steamed clams or mussels, crab, and shrimp. Cook until the shrimp are done, which will take no more than 3 or 4 minutes.

Distribute among deep plates or bowls and sprinkle with parsley. Provide forks as well as spoons. Serve with crusty French or Italian bread.

SCOTCHED CRAB SOUP

Serves 6

A healthy dollop of whiskey gives this delicious soup its unusual flavor.

1 pound cooked crabmeat
½ cup milk
2 cups heated milk
3 tablespoons butter
3 tablespoons flour
Salt and freshly ground black pepper
1 cup cream
⅓ cup Scotch whiskey
Finely chopped parsley

Put the crabmeat in a small saucepan with the ½ cup of milk, and heat gently. In another saucepan prepare a light béchamel sauce: Melt the butter, stir in the flour, and cook for a minute or so. Then gradually stir in the heated milk, and continue stirring until thickened. This should be a fairly light sauce. Season with salt and pepper. Stir in the cream and add the crabmeat. If too thick, thin with cream or milk. Bring to a boil. Taste for seasoning. Stir in the Scotch just before serving. Ladle into bowls and sprinkle with parsley.

SHELLFISH BISQUE

Serves 6

The term "bisque" applies almost exclusively to a rich, creamy soup of pureed shellfish, in which the shells provide part of the flavor.

1 medium onion, coarsely chopped
1 carrot, peeled and cut into julienne
1 stalk celery, cut into julienne
3 tablespoons olive oil
1½- to 2-pound live lobster, split
1 cup white wine
¼ cup cognac
½ cup rice, cooked in broth 45 minutes
1 quart fish stock
Salt and freshly ground black pepper
1 cup heavy cream
3 tablespoons butter
Cayenne pepper

Heat the oil in a pot, add the vegetables, and sauté them gently for 2 or 3 minutes. Then add the lobster halves and cook with the vegetables, turning occasionally, until the shell turns red. Add the wine and cognac, and simmer for another 6 minutes or until the lobster meat is just cooked through. Remove the lobster, extract the meat, and chop very fine. Break up the shells and put through a grinder.

Puree the ground shells, cooked rice, and vegetables in a food processor, and press through a fine sieve. Return to the pot, and add enough fish stock to make a thick soup. Season with salt and pepper. Add the cream and butter, and reheat. Finally add the chopped lobster meat and a dash of cayenne, and heat through.

VARIATION:

Substitute 18 crayfish or medium shrimp for the lobster.

LADY CURZON SOUP

Though named for the wife of the Viceroy of India, this soup is little known in England and is just as scarce in America, but it is one of the great standards of Curnian cuisine.

4 cups of the best canned turtle soup
2 egg yolks
1/3 cup heavy cream
1/2 teaspoon curry powder, or to taste
1/4 cup Madeira, sherry or cognac
Whipped cream
Minced parsley (optional)

Put the soup in a saucepan, bring to a boil, and remove from the heat. Mix the egg yolks with the heavy cream and curry powder. Very gradually stir 1 cup of the hot soup into the egg mixture to prevent the egg from curdling. Then stir back into the soup with the Madeira, sherry or cognac. Reheat gently while stirring, but do not allow to boil. The soup won't thicken but will become light and creamy. Pour into hot cups or bowls, and float a little whipped cream on top. If the cups are ovenproof put them under the broiler for a second to glaze the whipped cream. Otherwise just dust with minced parsley.

COLD SOUPS

COLD PEA-MINT SOUP

Serves 8 to 10

Split peas are usually associated with a ham bone and winter supper, so it may come as a surprise that they make a refreshing summery soup.

1½ cups green split peas
1 quart water
Salt
1 quart chicken broth
1 small onion, peeled and sliced
2 garlic cloves, crushed
1 sprig fresh mint
2 cups heavy cream

GARNISH:
Finely chopped mint leaves

Wash the peas and pick over them to remove any bits of stone. Place in a pot with the water and 1 teaspoon of salt. Boil 5 minutes, then remove from the heat and let stand for an hour. Return to the stove, add the broth, and bring to a boil. Then add the onion, garlic, and mint. Cover, and simmer over low heat until the peas are very tender. Taste for salt. Discard the onion, garlic, and mint. Puree the peas in a food mill or food processor. Chill thoroughly, preferably overnight. Stir in the heavy cream. Serve in chilled bowls or cups with a sprinkling of chopped mint.

CUCUMBER-YOGURT SOUP

Serves 4

One of the most refreshing of summer soups and one of the easiest to make.

2 cups fat-free chicken broth
2 medium cucumbers, peeled, seeded, and cut into strips
1 tablespoon finely chopped onion
Salt and freshly ground black pepper
Fresh dill, chopped
2 cups yogurt

GARNISH:
Paper-thin slices of cucumber

Combine the broth, cucumbers, and onion in a saucepan, and cook over low heat until the cucumbers are tender. Puree in a blender or food processor with 1 teaspoon chopped fresh dill and salt and pepper to taste. Cool. Blend with the yogurt, and taste for seasoning. Chill thoroughly. Float a few cucumber slices in each serving and sprinkle with additional chopped dill.

COLD SORREL SOUP

The French have long prized sorrel and use it in a traditional hot version of this soup, called Potage Germiny. Its lemony flavor makes it also ideal as a cooling hot-weather soup.

1 pound sorrel
6 tablespoons peanut oil
3 cups fat-free chicken broth
1 cup heavy cream
3 egg yolks
Salt and freshly ground black pepper

Wash the sorrel, strip the leaves from the stems, and bundle together tightly. Cut into thin strips. Heat the oil in a heavy saucepan, and gently cook the sorrel until wilted, about 5 or 6 minutes. Add the chicken broth, bring to a boil, and then reduce the heat. Simmer for 10 minutes. Remove from the heat and strain off the broth into a bowl. Puree the sorrel in a blender or food processor. Return the broth and sorrel to the saucepan, and blend.

Beat the cream and yolks together, and stir gradually into the sorrel and broth. Taste for seasoning. Cook over moderate heat until the soup begins to thicken. Do not allow to come to a boil. Cool and then refrigerate to chill thoroughly.

GAZPACHO

One of the most popular of all cold soups, Gazpacho has Spanish origins and many different interpretations, this being one from the West Coast.

3 pounds ripe tomatoes, peeled,
    seeded and chopped
2 cucumbers, peeled, seeded,
    and chopped
½ cup finely chopped green pepper
½ cup finely chopped onion
1 clove garlic or more, peeled and
    very finely chopped
2 cups chilled tomato juice
⅓ cup olive oil
3 tablespoons vinegar
Salt and freshly ground black
    pepper to taste
¼ teaspoon Tabasco

GARNISHES:
6 cubes frozen tomato juice
Tiny croutons of white bread
    (¼ inch square), browned in
    olive oil

This soup requires no cooking. Simply put all the ingredients (except for garnishes) in a large bowl, blend well, and season to taste. Chill thoroughly. Serve in bowls with a frozen tomato juice cube and a sprinkling of croutons.

COLD AVOCADO SOUP

Serves 4

Another soup that needs no cooking but merely a melding of flavors in hot chicken broth.

1½ cups very ripe avocado
1½ cups hot fat-free chicken broth
1 tablespoon fresh tarragon,
*   chopped, or 1 teaspoon dried*
¼ teaspoon Tabasco
1 tablespoon lemon juice
½ cup sour cream
½ cup heavy cream
Salt to taste
Chopped chives or fresh tarragon

Put the avocado through a food mill, or puree in a blender or food processor until very smooth. Stir into the hot chicken broth. Add the tarragon, Tabasco, and lemon juice. Allow to cool. Blend in the sour cream and heavy cream. Taste for seasoning. Chill thoroughly. Serve with a sprinkling of chopped chives or tarragon.

COLD PEACH-STRAWBERRY SOUP

Serves 10

The Scandinavians are the inventors of delicious fruit soups, which give a sparking start to any summer meal.

1 quart red wine
2 quarts strawberry syrup
2 tablespoons potato starch
2 whole cloves
1 piece cinnamon bark
Zest of 2 lemons
1½ pounds peaches, peeled and sliced
1½ pounds strawberries, washed and hulled

Combine all but 1 cup of the wine with the strawberry syrup in a saucepan, and bring to a boil. Mix the potato starch with the remaining red wine, and stir into the syrup. Reduce the heat and simmer for 2 to 3 minutes. Add the spices, lemon zest, peaches, and strawberries. Blend gently. Cool and then refrigerate to chill.

COLD CHERRY SOUP

Serves 8

2 pounds tart red cherries, pitted
2-inch piece of cinnamon bark or
    1 teaspoon cinnamon
2 cloves
¼ teaspoon salt
2 cups water
2 cups red wine
Sugar to taste
2 egg yolks, beaten

Put the cherries in a saucepan with the spices, salt and water. Cook until quite soft. Discard the cinnamon bark and cloves, and puree the cherries in a blender or food processor. Return to the saucepan. Add the wine and sugar to taste. Mix a couple of tablespoons of the mixture with the egg yolks, and stir this back into the saucepan. Cook over low heat, stirring constantly, until slightly thickened. Do not allow to boil. Cool and then put in refrigerator to chill.

VARIATION:

Omit the sugar and use port or a medium sherry instead of the wine.